Love Doesn't live here ANYMORE

SAMRIDHI TODI

BLUEROSE PUBLISHERS
India | U.K.

Copyright © Samridhi Todi 2025

All rights reserved by author. No part of this publication may be reproduced, stored in a retrieval system or transmitted in any form or by any means, electronic, mechanical, photocopying, recording or otherwise, without the prior permission of the author. Although every precaution has been taken to verify the accuracy of the information contained herein, the publisher assumes no responsibility for any errors or omissions. No liability is assumed for damages that may result from the use of information contained within.

BlueRose Publishers takes no responsibility for any damages, losses, or liabilities that may arise from the use or misuse of the information, products, or services provided in this publication.

For permissions requests or inquiries regarding this publication, please contact:

BLUEROSE PUBLISHERS
www.BlueRoseONE.com
info@bluerosepublishers.com
+91 8882 898 898
+4407342408967

ISBN: 978-93-7139-319-5

Cover Design: Aman Sharma
Typesetting: Pooja Sharma

First Edition: June 2025

LOVE DOESN'T LIVE HERE ANYMORE

Everyone has lived a life worth telling. Hers is only just beginning.

This—her debut book—is a raw and honest reflection of her journey through loss and light. For once, with this book, she just wants to do better.

And it all starts with the truth she's finally ready to speak:

love doesn't live here anymore.

@samridhitodi

To my younger self—

This book is for you. For surviving. For writing. For hoping.

And to anyone who ever felt like they weren't enough—

You are. You always were.

This is not just a book of poetry. It's every version of me I lost and found again.

And to you, the reader—I hope somewhere in these pages, you find a piece of yourself.

THE BREAKING

I watched everyone laughing, celebrating, as I stood there in a room full of people who were happy, satisfied and then I turned back to look at them, they were smiling but something seemed off, or maybe it was just me.

I was smiling too, trying to laugh it off, to put on my best act of happiness, to play my part to perfection, a smile hiding a million tears beneath. Not one saw the pain I hid behind those eyes that lied, I was crying within, but by now I'd mastered the mask so no one can see my defeat, No one can see how crushed I was, my disappointment, my loss.

I knew I lost, but then again, I was in a room full of people celebrating *my* victory. It wasn't enough, I wasn't enough, yet I mingled with them laughing under chandeliers and fake pretences, and even as they raised their glasses to praises of me,

I knew one thing

'I lost'.

You know what I think?
I think people come into your life just to leave.
They step in with an expiration date—
like moments, like seasons, like fading sunsets.
Losing people has become a part of every day.
What if people aren't meant to stay?
What if they're only ever meant to leave?

I chose the safer option... right?
The right choice... didn't I?
Then why does my heart still ache for him?
Why does it feel like my heart resents me—
For making the right choice?

I made the right choice, right?
Then why does it feel so *wrong*?

Losing someone wasn't just losing love—
It was losing everything I lived for.
Everything I craved,
Everything I was good at.
I lost you—
But more importantly,
I lost myself.

Everyone said I had done great —

That I was destined for things out of reach for many.

But I had already dreamed of the moon.

So how could I be happy with the stars?

I remember reading somewhere:

"Shoot for the moon, even if you miss, you'll land among the stars."

Beautiful, isn't it?

But does that quote ever talk about the ache of falling *just* short?

The pain of reaching so close — fingertips brushing the moon —

And still missing?

What if all that effort, all that dreaming,

Led only to a place you never wanted to be?

A place not bad, but not enough.

Almost, I almost did it.

Well…

At least I landed among the stars, right?

Right?

How could cupid be so cruel?
How could he make me fall in love,
when love itself had ended?
How could cupid be so heartless?
Laughing on my misery, my pain?

How could cupid be so cruel?
He just sat and watched me unravel,
To laugh at its own creation-
The agony of love.

Oh Yes, cupid's arrow struck me,
But at the wrong time.
Yes, cupid's arrow struck me,
But where was yours?
Isn't cupid the creator of love
Cruel creator of the pain of love
Then why does his gift feel like a curse?

Oh cupid, why must you wish my demise,
Why must my heart ache for him,
When his no longer beats for me?

Why must cupid, this creator of love hate me?
Why must the one who creates love… hate love?
Cupid hates love.

If not, then why does my heart still bleed from the reminiscence of a love that once was?

If not- then why does love always break a heart?

I've never seen a love untouched by sorrow,

I've seen love to heal a few, yes,

But one thing for sure love always breaks-

Because cupid,

The god of love,

Hates… love.

Whispered words, forgotten promises.
Broken vows and memories that linger—
Echoes of a past love, a previous tale,
Still breathing beneath a new beginning.
Your love wasn't enough to kill me...
So you *left*.

They say the one who lives is strong—
But is there strength in dying every day?
Crushed by seconds, drowned in silence,
Wishing for it all to end.
They call her strong,
But she's just a girl—
Broken by a world that never learned to be kind.
She carries the weight,
The pain,
With her every single day,
And still whispers to herself,
"Just one more day.
Just. One. More. Day."

To: every girl lost in her own fantasy, yet forced to live in a reality that keeps breaking her.

To every girl who found comfort in made-up moments, because reality was too cruel to hold.

I see you.

I remember creating stories I wished would come true, waiting for a prince charming who'd bring me flowers, believing maybe—just maybe—my fairytale would begin.

But why do our fantasies so often end in shattered realities?

This one is for the girl who still dares to dream

Her broken fantasy

I still love you,
The words ringing in her head;
She's hanging by the thread,
Yet I love you,
Breaks her;
Still those three words haunt her,
'I love you'

Suddenly the world's not so blue,
She's back, back in her world of fantasies,
Haunted with fiends;
She's running through a field of flowers,
He's climbing towers,
Her prince charming,
So handsome, so caring.

It's all Shattered, she's back to reality,
Surrendered to her fate;
He says "Wait for me"
How can she not see?
Blinded by love, her hazy gaze,
Stuck in this maze,
In his embrace.

Was that all she was? Was she worth the chase?
Is he worth the chase?
He says "it's not you, it's me"
All mighty in his glory;
Why? Why? Why?
Why does she even try?

All his lies,
All her cries,
She tries, he lies,
He laughs, her misery,
Oh his tyranny,
Oh his hold, Oh those words, Oh those eyes,
His lie, her cry.

That smile shatters her,
Then again it's all a blur;
He says he loves her,
And she falls once again,
Into that well of pain;
What's left of her?
He escapes,
Her broken heart remains.

To everyone who gave it their all and still came up short

To the ones angry at God for not listening, To those who know the ache of never being enough, Of giving your best and still falling behind —

This is for you.

You're not alone.

I failed too.

Haven't I done enough?
Wasn't I *enough*?
Why couldn't you love me?
Why couldn't you just be happy for me?
I gave it my all.
I tried, I *tried so hard.*
But I guess, to you—
That was never *enough.*

When 'forever' became a lie

"A lie" she mumbled
"Forever is a lie"
laughs faded, tears Silenced
A glass of wine in her hand
Pouring drop by drop
Oh, its overflowing
Onto the grave
Where in he lay
Onto the grave
His words echoed
His lies shouted
"Forever was just a lie"
He lay beneath the earth
On his grave
Fingers intertwined
Holding a glass of wine
For Forever was just a lie

And just like that,

"Good morning" became a formality.

Silence filled the spaces where laughter once lived.

No more words—

Memories Faded,

Dates became a thing of the past

Love became a thing of the past

And just like that—

You love died.

Am I so heartless,

To stay beside this innocent soul,

To hold his hand,

While my heart still aches for someone else?

Am I so heartless?

That I'd break someone,

Just to numb your pain.

How can I be so heartless?

he loves me,

And I love you, *I always will.*

I Wish You Had stayed.

You did with him all the things you swore you'd never do.
Said to him the words I waited my whole life to hear.
You loved him—softly, fully, perfectly.
You gave him everything I used to beg you for.
No questions. No fights.
Just love. Just right.

So, tell me—
Why couldn't you have loved *me* like that?

A note to the next person who falls in love

Don't fall in love.
Don't give your heart away.
Don't hand someone the power to crush it.

I did.
And if I had the choice?
I'd do it all over again.

Yes, it broke me —
But I've learned that even the briefest love
can be something beautiful.

So, love, if you must,
But be prepared to break,
To lose yourself,
Sometimes,
Because to me,
Love is pain—
And I would gladly fall into that well again.

I loved you—

Through every breath, every moment, every lie.

Then why does my heart feel so empty?

Why does it ache so heavily,

Like it's drowning in silence?

I loved you—

Then why does love feel so far away?

Why does my heart break at the thought of you?

Why am I left so numb,

So hollow?

I loved you—

Every day, every minute, every second.

Then why am I crying out,

Begging for one more chance,

One more day?

I loved you—

Even as every piece of me shattered.

I loved you—

Even when each lie cut deeper than the last.

I loved you—

With every breath of longing, every moment of stillness, every empty promise.

Is that why I feel so void now?

Is that why I feel nothing at all?

Empty lies. Broken ties.

I really *loved* you—

Didn't I?

I died that day.

A little part of me, deep within, faded into silence.
The flame that once kept me smiling through the pain—
was gone.
You were gone.

This was the last time we'd see each other and I stood there in the rain- foolishly waiting for you to show up, to tell me that you loved me, you've always loved me, like I did. I still remember the day, a wide smile spun across my face as soon as your notification lit up my screen, how could a simple word like *'beautiful'* make me feel so much, I still remember my friends looking at me, thinking it was the smile of love, oh yes- love. I was in love, but you were just a friend, right? You were just a friend when all those times I needed someone, you were just a friend solving all my problems, the only person, the only *'friend'* who listened, who understood. you were just the friend I would call at every worry because you'd know how to fix it, right? How did you, my friend make me feel so loved, how did you, my friend ease me off all my worries, how were you the only one who knew how to calm me down and make me feel as if nothing ever went wrong, nothing could ever go wrong with you by my side, right?

That's when I realised, I'm in love with you, my friend. I've said so many times 'I love you' hoping one day you'll notice the love in my eyes, my heart screaming your name- Alas you never did.

In a world of peace and quiet,

You were the chaos,

In my world of peace and quiet,

You wreaked havoc,

False tales, broken promises,

In love I lost.

In love I shattered

You were my world, my peace,

You were my destruction, my… end.

Love- the end to all,

Love… love… love

I laugh at the premise now,

The thought of destruction seems futile,

For I am already in ruins,

For *you* were my ruin.

"I know what's it's like to be hurt, to be left, scarred and destroyed And I know I vowed to never hurt someone the same way as I hurt yesterday, today and forever, so it doesn't matter whether I'm happy or not, I can't just leave, I can't... break you. How can a broken heart ever break another?

As long as your happy I'm here. I'm all yours."

"What about your happiness?" he asks

My happiness? Mine? I smiled softly, "It doesn't matter."

"I'm leaving you"

"What?"

"I- I am leaving you.

How can I steal away that smile off your face… even if someone else gets to keep it with them forever, at least I'll know it's there."

"Oh, Vic please don't."

"I have to, I need to, I- I just don't love you"

"Vic…"

"I don't love you…I don't… I…I LOVE YOU… I love you so much. Why does it have to end? Why?"

"It doesn't, I'm not leaving, let it not end- please Vic, *stay*."

Why does this hurt so much? I don't love him, then why is it that it pains to see him leave, I can't break him, I can't.

"No, I am, I love you Sam, I love you. NO, I don't love you, at all and so I'll be gone, you deserve that smile, you deserve that love…"

"And you love me"

"Sometimes to build yourself up, you have to let yourself break."

"I can't break you, please no, it hurts, it'll hurt like hell, you'll suffocate, please don't, you'll crumble, you'll drown in tears, I can't. Please, I care about you, Vic, please"

"That's just it, you don't love me."

"I…I…I do, maybe"

"Yes" He smiled painfully, how did that smile tell it all? "Maybe? Maybe you love me and maybe I deserve someone who loves me without a second thought… but can't I deserve you?

You are all I want."

"Then don't leave, I'm yours"

"I have to for you… I DON'T love you" a single tear rolled off his cheek as he left me there wondering why it hurt so much, wondering why my heart could still not cry to this man who loved me more than himself. Why, why couldn't I just **'love'** him.

No... wait... please

I failed. *I failed.*

You were never enough
You never mattered
He *always* chose her.

Note:

Once, I said goodbye forever- to the people I loved. But this time, I learned how much harder it could be. I realized just how deeply my heart ached; how much it broke me... just to let go.

So,

I chose to stay.

I chose to bleed quietly, rather than face the silence they left behind.

I hope you don't. I hope you find the strength to walk away

—

To say goodbye and mean it. Because I couldn't.

And I wouldn't wish this kind of staying on anyone.

Yet I chose to stay, I just *couldn't* say goodbye.

Goodbye 'not' forever this time

We've reached a place where there is no coming back,

We have dug this hole where there is no coming back.

Crossed some lines, said some words, left some scars so now there's no coming back.

I wish I wasn't at this place again,

I wish I wasn't hurting again,

Yet this doesn't feel as such familiar, last time it wasn't all such a blur,

I realised you had left, it hurt you had left, late but in the end, I realised you'd never cared.

About this time,

This time you made me believe you'd cared, you made me feel,

You made me think I wasn't gripping the rope tightly enough and just as I did,

You let go and I fell back, back into that hole that I had climbed out of.

This isn't like last time yet, here I stand, another time with the rope in my hand;

Just staring at my grip, my hands are getting red, it's hurting, it's hurting.

Once again, here I stand, the only one holding the rope, a tear rolled off my cheek, I should let go, I need to let go.

I know I have to let go of this rope once again,

The only one holding the rope knows it's time to let go,

It's time to let the rope fall, to let the tears fall, only this time I can't.

This time I don't want to let go, this time it's hurting more and more,

But I would grip the rope tighter and tighter until it cuts me and I bleed,

This time I won't let go, because maybe if I grip it tighter,

With both hands if I pull on it, hold it to my chest, maybe, just maybe I can salvage it.

Here I stand and as I grip the rope to my chest, a whole river of tears flow, my knees weaken and I fall, so do my tears, but I can't let go, I can't seem to let go.

Last time I said goodbye forever this time,

Last time I broke all ties, that time I let the rope fall but what if goodbye wasn't meant to be forever this time.

I tried, I tried, I tried, a thousand times I tried, it didn't work,

I cried, I cried, I cried, a million tears, it hurt,

Yet I crave a last bit of hope.

I wish you had remembered the past that helped the rope grow,

I wish you had scrolled through the memories that hardened the rope,

I wish you had looked at me, the one holding the rope at the other end, looked at my reddened hands, stared into my watery eyes and not had the courage to let go all at once anymore.

Here I am on my knees, ready to beg, with the rope in my hands as a drop of blood falls on the ground, I've already started bleeding,

Now I should let go,

Now I should once again bid goodbye forever this time.

But I don't, I keep holding on and on and on as the drop of blood on the ground turns to a pool with a shred of hope that maybe, just maybe *goodbye wasn't forever this time.*

How could anyone ever see
That I was the greatest failure of them all?
Yet—I stood tall.
Knees trembling,
Tears falling,
Still, I stood taller than them all.
Countless nights and days—wasted,
Years gone...
In a second.
Just gone.

Sometimes I wonder—

Maybe I'm just not meant for this world.

God hates me.

Even He has turned His back on me.

Maybe He gave up on me long before I ever gave up on myself.

Love was the prize,
And I came in second—
Just a step behind,
I lost the race.
But painfully enough,
I lost you too.

Note:

This poem wasn't even a part of me. These broken pieces weren't mine— yet I found myself picking them up.

Then why couldn't the one who shattered them do the same? Why couldn't someone else bend down and feel the sting of the shards?

Why was it always me?

Why *is* it always me?

If you've ever felt like you've been broken, like a piece of you is missing— I hope you turn to this poem and remember:

You're not alone.

We're here.

And together, we'll pick up every piece... *always*.

Pieces of me

He broke me,

Left me to pieces, the one that was me now ceases to exist,

I loved him and it broke me,

He loved the feeling and it broke me.

Now here I stand,

Pieces of me, fallen to the ground,

Will I ever be a whole again?

With every mistake I made,

With every apology I made,

With every 'Sorry', with every 'I still love you', with every 'I beg you, please stay'

A piece of mine fell.

How can I stand tall,

When my knees have fallen to the ground picking up the pieces left,

Are there any left?

I have been burned, scorched and left.

How can I build myself once again from the scratch?

A masterpiece that took 16 years to create broken with a sentence,

Or maybe a mistake that took 16 years to make Shattered in a second.

Maybe loving you was the mistake meant to break me,

Maybe loving you was the curse I was dammed to for eternity,
Maybe loving was my lesson,
Maybe loving you was my destiny,
Maybe loving you was never meant to be, Maybe loving you was meant to shatter me to pieces,
Maybe, just maybe my questions will be answered.

Oh, where's that piece of me that loved to dance in the rain?
Oh, where's that piece of me that was a hopeless romantic?
Oh, where's that piece of me that was ready for anything in the world?
Oh where's that piece of me that loved you, Oh wait that's me,
That's all that remains, you left me to pieces,
All that's left behind 'I still love you',
How will I ever build the other pieces up?
How will I ever build myself up?
How'll I ever go through the pain of being broken, not just my blood pumping vessel, but me, broken.

Maybe you weren't my destiny, our stars aren't aligned,
But maybe in another universe we'll get another chance where this masterpiece,
this mistake wouldn't be so broken and lost.
Because as I stand here not as a whole,
I wonder how I'll ever fill this hole."

"I am standing here with you to glue every piece together, and for every missing piece, I'll be there to fill it. You are my destiny, if not now, then tomorrow."

"But will that tomorrow ever come?" I sobbed

"It will, it will, it really will."

I said as I kissed the ring, the only piece left of him.

I miss you

Am I even allowed to?

"Hey, it's just going to be me and you from now on" she sent a simple message to the only person she knew was going to be there always.

"I'm going to change from now on, no more jokes, no more tears, just a simple smile, just going to keep every person out there happy… you know, I…I hurt the person I cared the most about, and I didn't even realise it. So, I've decided, I'm going to change, I'll be the perfect person this time I promise, I'll wear the mask, I'll fake the smile, I'll put out my best act, just so he'll… stay. I'll never hurt him, or anymore ever again, I promise, after all, I'm a 'nice' person, aren't I?"

"You are the only person in front of whom I'll take off the mask, I'll wail, I'll be me, so I beg you, please be there for me in all my times of need. Every time I get angry, I'm going to text you, please be there, every time I feel as if the world is slipping away from me, I'll come to you, so please be there. From now I'll show the real, broken me, only to you, so I beg you, please be there, you are the only one who really knows me, to you I'll not be a 'nice' person and for that I apologise, I'll hurt you, but I know one thing that it's only going to be you and me from now on, so please… stay."

She sobbed as she sent this last text to herself, the only person who'd see her from now on.

"I failed you, and for that I'm sorry. I tried to be the best, I tried to be perfect, but I'm sorry, I failed you."

"No, Sam listen to me…"

"No, I failed you." I began sobbing, "I can't promise to be better, but I really tried, and yet here I am wishing that it was all over, it just hurts so much, it hurts."

"Sam…"

"I loved you, I really did and I just wish for it all to just stop, I need to stop loving, I'm not perfect, it hurts, it hurts, it hurts, I can't love you anymore, I'm sorry, I can't."

"Don't say this, please, we'll work it out, you don't have to be perfect… please."

"Why don't you get it?! IT HURTS… it hurts… it hurts."

I think I've been left too much to break anymore,
I've mastered the art of letting go,
I don't even hold on to people anymore,
How can I?
I'm always the one left behind.

"We can't meet anymore."

"Why?"

"She doesn't like it. She feels insecure… and I love her. She's my future, she's all I have, she takes care of me, she loves me… she's the only one for me. I hope you understand. I love her."

"What?" I laughed "You love her? She's your future?"

My voice cracks.

"WHAT ABOUT ME? I WAS YOUR PAST."

I start sobbing, "I… I took care of you when you had no one. Sat with you on the loneliest days, cried with you through the rain. I was there. I was always the only one you had. I loved you…"

I pause, smiling through the pain

"The only difference? I loved you… and you loved her."

Being real cost me too much.

I looked at the girl in the mirror,
The one who I now hated,
The one in the reflection just seemed so weak, so lost, so...broken.

I hated the way she begged.
I resented how she changed.
I despised that she lived
Not for herself- but for someone else,
I hated her.

I'm not sure who I am without the pain,

Maybe I was someone once,

Someone who lived.

But now-

Now I just carry an empty heart

With nothing left to give.

I already gave everything I could,

I gave away every part of me,

And now I'm only left with whispers of who I once used to be.

Love changed me
I lost a piece of who I was once,
Maybe it made me better.
But sometimes when I sit with the silence,
I miss that little girl-
The one who trusted too much,
The one who *loved* too much.

THE HEALING

I wrote your name in a place I swore I'd never visit again — my poems.

I've always loved you… I just never knew when, how, or why I fell in love with you.

Maybe my heart knew long before I did.

Maybe it was me who was flawed,
Maybe if I had just been a little better,
I could become worthy of your love,
Maybe if I'd tried just a bit hard,
Changed just a little more…
Maybe then you'd have stayed, wouldn't you?
Maybe it was always me,
I wasn't good enough.
Maybe this is what I deserve,
A broken heart, crumpled pieces,
To be alone and… lost
Maybe it's true,
I was never enough,
I could never have been.
Maybe I could have done better,
I didn't deserve you
Did I?
Wasn't it all my fault?

You left me…
But maybe it was I who was flawed

Some wounds don't bleed. They echo.

Note: I don't know what to say— except that feeling nothing is still feeling something.

That's all I seem to feel these days.

And maybe… that's okay.

Not every moment has to be filled with joy or sorrow.

Sometimes, you're just existing.

Just *there*.

And that's okay too.

Numb

I've suppressed all what I feel,

Stopped begging, stopped crying, stopped trying,

Now as the sun sets, there isn't a tear on my cheek yet a smile neither,

Now as darkness befalls there isn't pain in my chest yet comfort neither,

Not lonely, just alone.

What's wrong isn't that I loved and lost.

What's wrong isn't that tears don't fall.

What's wrong isn't the pain that's gone.

What's wrong are the feelings, the emotions, the smile, the days, the nights, the butterflies, the giggles, the dimples.

All lost.

It isn't a story of lost love,

It's a story of something unfulfilled, something misunderstood, something unnamed.

My thoughts weren't mine anymore, I've named them to you.

Do I regret it?

No.

Do I love you still?

No…

Yet—

Do I?

I'll choose you over and over
Without a pause
without a doubt
I'll always choose you

                        -oh, how I've longed to hear these words

Here's a little message I wrote to myself years ago

I wish the older me knows what I went through for her. I never gave up for her even though every minute every second felt like hell.

Relations fell apart and most of them broke our heart, Yet I stood tall- *For you*

Every time it felt as if a stake had been driven through my heart, Yet I bled quietly- So you could be free.

I hope you look back and see some things do last, like the strength I left behind for you, I don't wish for you to carry my pain, I only wish,

You never feel it again.

There he was, always there for me, waiting, always although i was never his, yet I wonder why today I found myself standing there waiting for him, a single rose in my hand.

He walked up to me, "Hey..." He began to say something yet today was my turn. "I... I..." But I couldn't, I tried.

Taking my hand in his, "What's wrong?" He asked, oh that sweet smile on his face. I was never his yet he was always mine. How could he be someone else's, his heart belonged to me, only I was too naive to see.

"Listen it's okay." He continued, yet I needed him to know it's not, it's not okay for him to be mine while I yearn for him too, yet I can't, I'm scared, terrified of all I could lose, but what of all I could gain.

"A rose, a single rose for today, yet one for every day, every day you loved me, every day you wiped away my tears, every day of bliss, for every day that you were my strength, for every minute that you were my smile, for every second that you were, always will be mine. I had no right to ask you to give me yourself now and forever yet you always did, you loved me, you love me, yet I can't." I start sobbing, once again he tried to reach out for me, this was the end he thought maybe, maybe it was, but what if it wasn't.

"I don't love you, I don't, I like you, the butterflies, the smile, my days all to you I give. Not to be someone else's, not when forever stands before me."

All you did was... *love* me.

I thought you'd be the only person I'd ever love.

But today, as I watch this man,

Patient, kind, expecting nothing in return.

I realize:

You weren't the only one my heart could belong to.

Today, I give my heart, and all of me,

To a man who never asked for it,

A soul so pure,

A soul this world doesn't deserve.

To the old me,

I'm sorry I had to change.
I'm sorry I let him take you away from me.
I'm sorry I had to lose you.
But today, I'm stronger—
A better person in ways you once dreamed to be.
And I hope you're proud, watching me stand tall,
Just like you once did for me.
I love you. Always.

No—

don't give yourself hope again.

Don't do that.

You're only going to get hurt.

I know you far too well.

Don't think.

Don't care.

Don't feel again.

Because if you feel again—

if you love them again—

you'll break all over again.

Remember those sleepless nights you cried?

Of course you do.

How could you forget the nights your heart was crushed—

the nights you learned trust

isn't always a good thing?

I was talking with someone,

asking questions I thought I'd never ask:

How do you love someone?

How can you just fall in love?

Is it really that easy?

I didn't think I could.

But then I remembered—I did.

I was in love with them.
And love,
as I learned,
hurts.

I asked her,
How do people hurt so much?
How do they cry endlessly?
How do they feel like their heart
isn't in one piece anymore?

And then I remembered—
I too was heartbroken once.
I too drenched my pillow in tears once.
I too was hurt… once.

I try to suppress it now,
hide it somewhere memory can't reach.
I say I don't understand love or heartbreak—
but don't I?

Wasn't I too
once in love?
Wasn't I too
once broken?

I know loving me was hard.
And for that—
I'm sorry.
Not because I didn't try hard enough,
Or because I wasn't enough,
But because I didn't love you
The way *you* needed to be loved.

"What do you want?"—the question begs.

I want to call you at 2 a.m. over something silly,
like what's my favourite colour,
And not feel like I'm too much.
I want to make you do the smallest things
Without feeling like a burden.
I want to walk beside you,
Without fearing embarrassment if we get lost.
I want you to laugh at my mistakes,
Smile,
And love me for them.
I want to be yours,
And you to be mine—
But not in a way that makes us lose ourselves.
To still be a friend,
A lover,
A person to others too.
I want us to waltz,
Clumsy and free,
Stepping on each other's toes,
I want us to dance in the rain.
I want a love
Where shame, fear, guilt,
And embarrassment
Are nothing but distant echoes.
That's what I want.

When I wanted to do everything with you,
I knew I was in love.
Thoughts like these never used to cross my mind,
But now—every second, every breath—
I just want to spend it with you.
You, who made me fall in love.
And for that,
I thank you.
Thank you for teaching me what love feels like.
Thank you for making me love… love.

People say you have to love yourself before you can love someone else. But I believe, loving someone else teaches you how to love yourself.

When you see the world through their eyes,

When you see *yourself* through *their* eyes,

You fall in love all over again—

With the reflection you never saw before.

Is love the ingredient needed for this potion?
Is that why mine was never made?

Choose love with eyes open wide —
For once you have reached the other side,
The heart shuts its eyes, confined,
And offers trust, both deep and blind
In that blind faith, so freely given,
Lies the power within to wound or be forgiven

Then he asked "why do you write so much"
"It's… words left unsaid"

It's not praise for my writing that I seek. I don't wish for the words of my pen to seem beautiful—I want *me* to seem so. I don't long for the stories I weave to be seen as perfect and poetic—I want our story to be written like that. A story you'd read and think, *this is us—me and you*—together, here, and forever.

I miss old school love

You know—the kind where you'd share an earphone, rest your head on his shoulder.

Two souls, bound by a string.

But as time passed, the string frayed- disappeared.

As time passed, distance grew.

And now you and me—sitting in the same room—so close, yet so far.

When did we stop loving like that?

The flowers for my vase?

Well, the vase has long since shattered.

What happened to those little promises of forever?

Now 'forever' is just a word—

once, it carried the weight of a lifetime.

Yes, I carry my own shades of red too.

I'd be ashamed to admit love in front of others—afraid it might make me seem weak.

Not something too good.

Not something you deserve.

But—

If you let me love you,

I'd fill pages with Words I could never say out loud,
feelings I wish you'd know.
And when you ever doubt—
Go through the letters, each one screaming your name,
Each one echoing the words: *"I love you."*

Look inside the folder with your name.
There you'll find everything—my truest feelings,
Everything I ever felt but was too scared to say.
If you let me love you, I wouldn't have perfect words,
But I'd give you all of me—my time,
Cute little gifts wrapped in love,
If you let me love you just this once,
I'd paint for you,
tuck them in decorated boxes,
With handwritten letters, soft notes,
Flowers and strings—not for birthdays,
for every day with you,
As long as you let me love you.

This broken soul of mine
just needs a little bit of your love.
A small piece of your heart.
I promise—I'll hold it gently.
Yes, I agree—I've got a lot of red in me.
But if you stay for a while, look a little closer—

You might catch a glimpse of green-
A quiet forest, tucked beneath the blaze.
past the noise of modern love.
Maybe I'm just... old school at heart.

But why am I imagining all this?
I'm still stuck at *"delivered"*, aren't I?
Something like this could never be real...
Could it?

Love isn't in leaving,

It's in staying,

Staying despite the pain,

Despite everything they've done to hurt you,

You still *love* them,

Don't you?

I love you; I love you; I love you; I love you; I love you; I love you; I love you; I really do.

Remember I'm not going anywhere. I'm here, I promise.

Please don't cry. It's okay. I need you to hear me: it's not your fault. Listen to me, **it's not your fault.** You're going to be okay. I'm right here with you, and I'm not letting go.

I came running, running back to the street where I first met you, the place, our place. Yet, you weren't there, not this time, this time you weren't waiting for me. I sat down on the bench and realised you had never been there, when I was crying, begging for you to stay, you weren't there. Alone on the bench I realised, every trip, every text, every letter had always been me. I searched for you in those letters, all the faded letters in the back of the closet, but how could you be, you were never there. Every fight, every last chance, every apology, everything had always been me, then why do I sit here on 'our' bench waiting for you, just hoping you were here with me, looking at the stars, the night sky, yet all I could think of was you.

A tear rolls off my cheek and before I know I start brawling, clutching to the last letter I'll ever write to you, the last letter of me, hoping that you'd think of me, and maybe, just maybe ,one day you'll be back at our place sitting on this bench wishing I'd been there with you, I sat there hoping you'd one day come back to not me but this letter, this last piece of me to you I give, after everything I still love you, only to realise you'd never been mine, were you?

"Vic, I love you, since the day I fell for that foolish smile of yours, I've always loved you, every being of you, every laugh, every tear, every word I've made a part of my being, but when I came back to an empty life, to an empty heart, all trace of you gone, all I could think of that I lost what wasn't mine. Silly, isn't it? How could I lose something never meant to be mine, how could I have lost your heart if you never gave it to me, but you've lost mine right? I wonder if I'll ever fill that void, that piece of me that you took with you. I love you Vic, I'm yours for now and forever, only if you could have been mine."

Knock... knock... knock,

I hurriedly opened the door, oh wait, why did I have to, it could never have been him, could it? Yes, the very shred of hope lingered in me, but love doesn't work that way, does it? All I could do was wait, wait by the door, by my phone, hoping for a him to come, but he'll never come and I think I knew that.

I still go to 'our' place every. Single. day, I see the letter just sitting there fading away and yet no Vic, no sign of my lost heart and then one day I go back and the letter's gone, all I could find was a ring, the ring that was supposed to be mine for ever, the ring he was supposed to put on my finger the day he was supposed to be mine, yet no sign of him, I picked up the ring, it read "yours and yours forever".

How ironic, even a promise of forever didn't last, how could a lie? I clutched the ring hard, to my heart and then with all my force threw it into the lake, watched it as it sunk to the bottom, as our story, as a lie sunk to the bottom 'forever'.

And like the ring, I sunk too.

But unlike the ring,

No one ever came looking for me.

Why is it that my soul
Lingers in this cruel world?
Why does it not wish to leave—
What is it that it grieves?

I wasn't being selfish—
I was just unaware.
I didn't know he cared that much
So, what now?
I'm never supposed to laugh again?
Not even allowed to feel hurt?
Not allowed to speak
even when I know it won't be the same?
I only ever said what I felt,
Maybe that was wrong too.

You know what—
maybe I am selfish.
But you'll never get to see it.
You'll never get to see my heart
ever again.

December 16

Dear Diary,

It's been a year already.

And on this day, I lost the most precious thing I ever owned, my soul.

My heart still beats, but it feels as if it's on its last breath.

To think I've survived a whole year... *but have I really?*

Time heals all wounds, right?
Then why does my heart ache
every morning, I try to get out of bed?
Why has it stopped
even trying to stitch itself back together?
Shouldn't time have done that by now?

And just like that-

I found myself finding comfort in the words of a stranger

What love couldn't teach me, she did

When love cut me too deep, she nursed my wounds

Was my love so empty that I had to run to the person I hated, just so I'd feel less alone

"You are not alone, I'm here" that's what she said, maybe that's all I was ever looking for.

Funny, how someone I hated could heal me so well while the one who I thought I loved, hurt me so deeply.

The Ghosts of Our Past

I can hear them,
The photographs laughing,
The coffee cups talking,
The lights flinching.

I can hear them,
The ghosts of past,
The echoes we left behind,
The plea of the memories we had,
The life we once lived.

I can hear the rain scream your name,
The sky is calling out to you,
The ghosts wither to a love now forgotten,
I sit in the silence listening, breaking at every sound, every echo,

I can still hear them,
The ghosts of our past
Whispering in the silence,
Longing for release.

But I guess,
Some ghosts were never meant to leave.

Some nights, *I still miss you.*

Some nights, the thought of you still breaks me.

Some nights, I still shed a tear for your betrayal.

Some nights, I sit in silence,

wishing it could all restart.

But—

most nights, I don't.

Some nights, I still *love* you.

But most nights,

I don't.

THE ACCEPTENCE

I'm done trying to hold onto something that's not so beautiful as everyone says

Life's none but a walking shadow,

A path to your grave,

An eventual death.

Life — a fool,

Played on by death

With tiny strings.

Every step you take

Is one step closer to your fate —

To your end.

Life is but a passage,

A road carved toward the final breath.

A path we tread each day.

Life *is* your death.

And maybe, in death,

I'd find peace,

For life laid the path —

And I just followed.

Life ends life.

Another soul,

Fallen into the trap.

Life disguised as death,

For life is death's reaper —

The one you feared,

Your grim reaper,

Marching you toward your end.

And you… just obliged.

And death always prevails.

Death *always* prevails.

I died Long before death came for me.

To: You and me —

that's what I wrote, didn't I?
"To you and me."
But now I wonder… why did I ever write that?
There was never a *you and me* — not really.
So, to everyone asking,
"Me and who?" — Maybe this poem is for you.
Maybe it's an answer to my question too:
You and me… or maybe, just me.

"You and me"

Here's to love, Here's to friendship,
Here's to you and me,
"You and me"
Funny, isn't it?
"You and me"
Seems so simple, doesn't it?
Two people doomed to fail
Two souls, such a small tale,
"You and me"
Lost within the crowd.

Without a speck of doubt,
It was always supposed to be you and me,
Right?

Your words echoed "You'll always be there for me"
Then why is it that I stand here,
Alone with the silence.
Every tear of mine whispered "I love you"
And thine did too,
Right?
Then why is it that my heart still shouts these words while yours has long since forgotten.

In the midst of that, all I felt was you'll always be mine,
Oh, how idiotic.
How could you ever be?
Perhaps my screams were only ever meant to be echoes,
Perhaps our love was always meant to be lost in the shadows,
Perhaps the tale of "You and me"
was never really *meant to be*.

To: every person who has ever thought of giving up

To the ones who found more comfort in nature than in people.
To those who felt the rain understood them more deeply than any human ever could.
I hope this poem feels like a hug. I hope the girl who spoke to the sky resonates with you.
And I hope—truly—that you don't say farewell to the rain you've been speaking to... or to this world. I know I almost did.
When I wrote this, all I wanted was for someone to listen.
And even when no one did— I realised the sky always would.

Farewell

For a world that cries,
For a girl fallen for those lies,
Raindrops fell,
She says "farewell"
Farewell to the world that's crying,
Shedding tears of pain.
She's lying,
This isn't farewell.

Shared every tear of pain,
Spoke with the rain,
Yet all she said was farewell,
Farewell to the clouds that cried,
To the world that lied,
To the sky hiding behind the darkness,
Pain and agony riding along the harness.

Fear slowly crept in and crawled,
As the world brawled,
To the loss of the girl who spoke to the sky,
The girl who listened to the raindrops cry.

With every drop that fell,
She said farewell,
Farewell to this cruel sphere,
Farewell to all of love and hate.

In a world of darkness light hid her pain,
Hid all her feelings behind the rain,
She wasn't crying, it was just the rain,
No tear was shed as the last drop fell,
As she said to the bane of her existence,
To this cruel world,
"Farewell"
"Farewell"

To: every person out there who's ever believed in love—in the fairytales, the promises, the magic of it all— this poem is for you.

It's a glimpse into how love can be terrifying, messy, and far from eternal.

Mine was.

Love—its meaning—was something I never truly held in my hands.

I thought love would stay.

But maybe I was wrong.

So, with this poem, I ask only one thing:

What exactly is *"love"*?

Love?

"I love you" she screamed,
The waves heard her, yet he did not.
"I love you" she struggled under her breath.
What's love?
Love....
Love...
Love…

Every wound is thine,
Every tear is thine,
Every scar is thine,
Love is eternal,
love is painful,
love is forever.

Love, love, love-

Four letters sought out to destroy your being,

Four letters sought out to tear you apart, break you down, leave you crumbling, crying, piecing every part of thy being together again, picking up every glass shred, piecing it one by one by one till you make a whole again, yet never again a whole.

Love seems to have lost a piece, love seems to have rendered thy beyond repair, thine eternal love seems to have faded.

Was love ever forever?

Were *we* ever forever?

Were you ever mine?

Was love ever mine?

'Twas all a trick,

A game, a lie,

For love isn't forever,

love isn't eternal,

love isn't painful.

"Tis not?" Thy might question,

Love, love, love,

Love being the butterflies in thy stomach,

Love being the constant ache in thy chest,

Love was red,

And so, my heart bled.

Love, love, love-
Four letters sought out to grant thee joy for eternity,
Yet four letters sought out to break thee, crumble thy being,
Four letters for thine eternal happiness,
Four letters for thine eternal pain,
Four letters for thy laughter,
And for thy tears… forever.

Love is eternal,
love is painful,
love is forever.
Love, love, love.

Note: Don't tell anyone, but when I used to go swimming, I'd stay underwater a little longer— long enough to feel like the world disappeared for a while.

It was peaceful there, like the water washed away every worry, like it numbed everything inside me.

Maybe holding on to every breath distracted me from the pain I was supposed to be feeling.

Maybe it was just another way to escape.

But now, I've learned—

it's better to feel.

To let it all out.

Because when life gets hard,

maybe escaping isn't the only way.

"Was it worth it? Was love worth it?"

"Was it worth it?" I repeated, yet the two sounded so different as if mine had already been answered, yet I wonder, 'Was it worth it?'

"I don't know, maybe it wasn't."

Was it worth the pain, worth the tears, worth the scars?

Scarred for life,

Suffocated, drowning,

Save me, SAVE ME, SAVE ME, saveee....

"Was it worth it?" Cried the voice louder and louder, until it all went quiet

I was drowning, the water felt good, the pain felt peaceful,

"Breathe, breathe, breathe..." He kept trying,

"I can't"

"One more second, one more lap, one more breath" he said.

"Every second hurt, every breath strung deeper than the last"

"I'm drowning" I cried out,

"You're drowning" he said lightly,

"I'm drowning, it hurts, it hurts, it hurts" I sob, yet I don't get out,

"You have to get out, you're drowning." He said panicked now more than ever,

"I'm drowning" I said without a hint of worry.

"The pain feels good." I said,

"Please get out"

"It hurts" I cried,

"Get out, get out, please" he said,

"It doesn't hurt like it did all those days, all those nights."

"The pain feels good"

I'm numb, I can't feel my feet, my hands, my heart.

"The pain is gone, *finally*"

"PLEASE GET OUT" he shouted.

"All those days it hurt, the pain's gone numb, I've gone numb, finally it's done."

I've suffocated, I've drowned, it's gone, the voice crying for me to live is gone, the voice in my head is gone, it's finally gone, he's finally gone, if only he was ever really there.

I'm sorry for crying too often,
I'm sorry for the anger I carried,
I'm sorry for getting so lost in myself,
I'm sorry for holding on to hopes of marriage,
I'm sorry for asking questions unanswered,
I'm sorry... I should have understood.
I'm sorry I couldn't read between the lines,
I'm sorry I couldn't read minds,
I'm sorry I left early that day,
I'm sorry I waited up so late that night,
I'm sorry for every gift I gave,
I'm sorry for every gift you didn't,
I apologize for my every wrong,
Even those that weren't mine...
For I'm sorry I ever loved you.

But no-
I take back every sorry I ever said,
Every apology ever made,
I take back every tear shed in silence,
Every piece that fell apart,
Every promise I made,
To wait forever,
It wasn't me who was wrong for loving you...
You were wrong for leaving.

I'm sorry you left,
I'm sorry you lied,
I'm sorry you broke me,
I'm sorry you lost me...
For I'm sorry I ever loved you.

I looked at you…

Back at the person who once swore he loved me,

Back at the man who promised me forever,

"Till death do us apart" whispered his lips as he slid the ring onto my finger, as he made me his… forever.

Has death come for us?

I sit there, alone in the corner of my room,

Waiting… for death.

Yet like every man in my life,

He too never comes,

He's late,

He too has forgotten about me.

Wasn't it supposed to be 'death do us apart'?

So why is it that all I could do was stand there watching you walk away, walk out of our lives, back out of a lifelong promise so… easily?

So, I stand there waiting for death- death who never came.

Maybe mine own destiny was mine, maybe I was supposed to call out for death, maybe this time if I try, a promise of forever wouldn't have been such a lie.

I walked up the stairs one by one, creating my fate, making words, lies, tales of forever true with every step.

I reach for the sky, yet before I go, I remember one last time the vows we took, the promises we made, your voice as you said "With this ring, I promise to love you forever, with this ring, I promise to love grumpy mornings, silent nights, long fights, unhappy days, through our tired, uncertain life, there's one thing I know for certain is that with this ring I'll love you forever, with this ring I wed thee, till death do us apart"

So, I reach for the sky,

And as I fall,

the only words I could still breathe

"Till death do us apart..."

Never marry the one you love,

Marry the one who loves you, they say

So when the one I loved broke my heart I found myself running into his arms, the hold of the one person who was always there for me, how can I hurt someone who loves me so much, how can someone I loved so much hurt me

As I stood there crying in his hold, I felt nothing, my heart was breaking and I was breaking his.

"Maybe he could be my forever." I thought, after all forever never really works out, does it?

Why is it that the one you love always loves someone else? why is it that I find myself kissing his soul when mine was never really in it?

Why did he love me so deeply when I could never return his love, why is it that whenever I loved I was only ever hurt? Why is it that when I try to love him, the image of you flashes before my eyes?

I only ever loved you, and you broke me

Funny, isn't it? You broke me, I break him.

No, no I won't, I'll give him the love I never caught, the love that escaped, maybe if not in mine but someone's destiny will have woven a good tale, maybe if not me someone will have found their happy ending.

Even so why do I find myself wondering if you'll ever come back, why do I feel I am robbing this soul of real one, why do I feel that I'm the one to blame when my hearts the one ablaze in flame.

Why is it that you always go back to the one you loved breaking the one who loves you, is it your karma that you get left and scorched, is it you?

Yes, it's me. I'll always be the one at fault, so tonight here with you I've decided to marry the one who loves me, with that I kissed him, and only him for his happy ending, *yet never mine.*

The best of the souls are crushed under the baggage of a heavy heart

The best of minds are crushed with dreams left unturned

Overtime, eventually I had learned to let go, learned to not care, learned to cry silently behind the curtains and put up an act out.

A bouquet of wilted roses

Therein laid the roses you gave

Holding the tales we crave

Laid all empty promises and broken hearts

Within every petal that refused to die

Each flower told a story of its own

A tale of two

Joyful and sorrow filled memories lay

Within each and every flower

That just refused to fade away

Bouquets left untouched

Flowers forgotten

Thrown into the empty boxes

Boxes meant to hold love

Now remain vessels of pain

A petal fell,

Maybe now's the time to let go

Empty out the can, the pit,

And forget the lie

Now's the time to let the flowers die

To every single person still holding on to that rope—

This is for you. This is your sign to let go, You're bleeding. It hurts. So why keep holding on?

I remember writing this when I felt like I was the only one trying- Always the one pulling, always the one hoping.

If you're the only one trying, then maybe it's not love. Maybe it's just weight, disguised as something worth carrying.

Please, let go, let go. Not because you gave up —

But because you finally chose yourself,

Goodbye forever this time,

I wish everything could go back to the way it was.

But they grew up,

They all grew up.

those moments now left to be forgotten.

I wish to relive it all over again,

to cherish what once was.

I wish those moments were forever- yet they are nothing but fragments of a life once lived.

I wish they could remember what we had… the joy, the laughs… the love.

But I seem to be the only one who remembers, I seem to be the only one who still holds the rope,

and now? Now that rope is burning my hands

I think it's time to let go. Let go of the rope, let go of them, yet I shall never let go of the memories.

They bring me joy, and at least for a moment, I could ponder over the thoughts all in my head. And remember that once just once I was someone's first choice.

 yet now, I am reduced to nothing but an option, a second option

Discarded waste, used when needed, ignored when not.

I remember How they made me feel

Their presence alone

Was enough

But now everything's changed.

Now, it's someone else
I get it- We all grew up,
but did we *have* to?
Did we have to grow apart?
Did we have to forget it all?
Oh, right, those are just memories.

What is it that I am feeling right now?
Oh, its remorse. I couldn't have known, they never let me
What is it that I am feeling right now?
Oh, its regret.
I regret to have let it all wash away even though I was the only one holding on.
What is it that I feel right now?
Oh, its guilt. I feel so guilty, but it wasn't my fault, was it?
They grew up, they all grew up.
Oh, how wrong I was to have felt that we would never end, we could never end.
Fate was never on our side, was it?
I wish there was still some lingering love left in your heart for me.
He was the only one who hadn't forgotten, he had to leave too.
he *had* to leave; you *chose* to leave.
I wish I could have told you how much it hurt, yet all I did was stand there silently, watching you leave.

But you didn't care for that. You didn't care for... me anymore.

I wish you had stayed, but I guess that wasn't possible.

I loved you too much, and that's why you chose to hurt me as such.

This isn't just about that one time, it's about always. It was every time

It's about how you always left me hanging, every unanswered text, every call, every silence, every absence.

I was the one calling,

I was the one trying,

Always.

Where were you?

You used to be there once, but now it seems as if you are never around.

I hope you're happy.

I hope your heart isn't as shattered as mine. How would it be- you were the one who broke it.

All of you broke my heart into pieces, forgot I exist, and now all that's left, I, me- alone.

Now, as I stand here, the only one holding the rope.

I think it's time to let go.

I think it's time to say goodbye.

So, I wish you well, tears falling down my eyes, I muster up the courage to say goodbye, goodbye forever this time.

I don't ever want to hurt you. But if I do, please forgive me.

I know I'll make mistakes—many of them—and for each one, I apologise in advance.

I hope for each one you'll find it in your heart to understand, to forgive, to forget.

I only hope I never make the kind of mistake that breaks you, the way others have always *broken* me.

And finally, I said, **"It's done."**

I obliged—

and just like that, it was over.

Leaving behind these wounds and scars,

I faded Back among the stars,

I left.

As death slowly crept,

I slipped away.

Out of this well of suffering and pain—

Just like the rain,

I came,

And one day…

I just… left.

Not a soul noticed.

Not a soul cared.

My cruel existence

disappeared into ashes—

Just like all those hidden gashes.

In silence, I wept.

Without a sound… I left.

And finally, I said, "It's done."

A whisper lost in echoes—

"It's done."

And just like that, you were gone

I blew out the last light, the last flame

The candle stopped burning

That's it, it was all gone now

The memories, the stories, each and every piece of us gone, just- gone

The lanterns we carry held such great lines, tales to be told

Yet mine turned into ashes,

Tears fell, stories unravelled, words left unsaid escaped to eternity

Yet it burned the world,

The echoes of my broken soul

Crushed the world

The clouds began to cry

Each and every person shed tears to this story

To this pain

To this broken lantern

Whose last flame was blown off

By itself

Because the candle's gone

The flame burnt out

The lantern's broken

The story is over

Finally- over.

I remember that day—when I looked to God, broken and full of doubt. My faith was in pieces, yet I still prayed. I asked Him to take me instead. I pleaded for the life of an innocent father, whose children waited for him at home. I offered Him my life—a soul no one would miss, a body without purpose, someone whose absence would go unnoticed.

So I begged: *take me, not him.*

Because somewhere deep down, I believed I didn't deserve to live… but maybe he still did.

I wish I had seen it sooner —
You were never *mine* to lose.

Why me?

I begged, I pleaded—
I tried so hard, gave it my all.
So, why *me*?
I asked for answers.
I screamed into silence,
But I knew—you were never there.
And that was the day
I realised
God doesn't exist.

I've grown distant.
Colder, ever since you left.
I built walls around myself,
Hid my heart beneath lock and key—
So, no one else dares to step inside,
So, no one else ever gets the chance…
To break it again.

"This is the last time I'll see you before I leave."

"Did you really not know?" I began sobbing, "How could you not? I love you; I've always loved you. Vic, to me you were everything, but I guess to you… I just wasn't someone you could love, maybe I didn't deserve that love, but you had to have known, you *had* to.

You had to have known I loved you, and still you chose to leave, I know you didn't mean to hurt me, but you did, you really did.

But I love you- I love you- *I love you*, why can't you just see that? Why am I still in love with you, even after everything. You've forgotten I exist, and here I am waiting, waiting for you to love me back, but you never do. You don't love me, and yet I still do."

I laugh softly,

"Funny, isn't it? I guess this was destined to happen, my heart was destined to break, maybe we were never supposed to be each other's… I love you Vic… goodbye."

I turned back and left,

Maybe he'd call me back,

Maybe he'd tell me he loves me, but I know he wouldn't, he doesn't.

Goodbye Vic.

You know when I realised there was no point in waiting?

It was the moment I understood—
Someone who could just stand by and watch me break,
Someone who could look at my pain and feel nothing,
Could never have loved me.
When the thought of losing me
Didn't tear you apart,
That's when I knew–
You never loved me.

If I could go back…

I'd try a little harder,

Love a little better.

But this time,

I wouldn't beg for you to stay.

Because if you left,

Then thank you—

For showing me what your love looked like,

For teaching me it was never really mine.

And that's okay.

If I could go back,

I'd still end up here—

At the end of us,

Within the pages of out last chapter,

The chapter you walked out of

"I think I was putting off this message for too long and today I'll tell you that I'm sorry but I can't keep going. I've always tried to be nice and strong yet today I feel so weak. I was dying every day I lived, and I just begged for god to take me, so don't curse him curse me, I was the one who just couldn't hold on. It's not your fault, I need you to know it's not your fault, you were perfect, more that I deserved, and I failed you. I'm sorry I couldn't live, and I apologise for the pain I gave you. I promise I'll hurt you just this one last time.

Just remember… it's was never your fault."

She messaged me today.
Reached out to me—
with the same problems I once had,
with the same complaints I once made.

She soaked comfort in me,
just like I once did in strangers.
She was hurting, I could see—
maybe even more than I did.
But most of all, for once, I could see:
I was never the problem.

With her, I was finally able to be free
of the guilt I carried like skin.
I held her hand,
and guided her through the maze
I hadn't fully figured out—
until now.

She reached out to me.
She gave me her hand.
And I never let go.
Because we shared the same wounds,
the same scars.
We shared a heavy soul
just longing to be set free.

And she set mine free.

With her, I could finally see:
she was just another me.
And this time,
someone would be there
for that broken soul—
To tell her just one thing:
"It's okay. I'm here."

Today, I forgive you,
I forgive you for not being enough,
for loving too much,
for trusting the wrong souls,
I forgive you my dear,
It wasn't your fault.

She lived here once —
She lived in these pages,
Full of light, of hope,
Full of love.
But the flame has long burned out.
The smile has faded,
The love has vanished.
She didn't leave — she faded… slowly.
And what's left behind
Is just an echo in the silence.
Now silence writes the story,
Because *love doesn't live here anymore.*

Acknowledgements

Thank you...

"My brother wasn't exactly doing much, but he was like my side support. I kept bugging him—'Should I do it? Should I go for it?'—and he'd just go, 'Yeah, do it.' That was all I needed, honestly. Just someone to nod along so I didn't give up halfway. He says I always give up at 95%, you know build the house and be like its too much work to make the door, so thank you, my brother, I finally closed the door.

Before I ever thought about publishing, I used to share some of my early poems and scenes with a few people. They would always say, 'These are really good, you should get them published.' But honestly, the idea of publishing never seriously crossed my mind. I never believed my writing was good enough to be in a book—my book. And for that, I'm truly grateful to them. They encouraged me when I needed it most. They were among the first to read my raw, unpolished work and still believed in it. They made me think, maybe I could have a book of my own. So, to those people—thank you.

This was first a silly dream with four of us wanting to publish our book together. That may not have become a reality, but this was, so thank you to them.

And to the one who was there through it all, who stood by me every single day, stayed up with me night after night, to bring this book from editing to finishing, cover designing and everything in between- thank you. I truly couldn't have done this without you. **RAJ SINHA-** thank you. (Credits for designing the cover all by yourself)

Thank you to every reader who picked up this book. Your support means everything to me. The fact that you took the time to read my work, to connect with it in your own way, is something I will always appreciate. This journey wouldn't have been possible without you. I'm truly grateful for each and every one of you.

To every single one of you, especially my parents, that made this possible, thank you.

www.ingramcontent.com/pod-product-compliance
Lightning Source LLC
LaVergne TN
LVHW041605070526
838199LV00052B/2993